Raymond Knister
and His Works

Joy Kuropatwa

Raymond Knister (1899–1932)

JOY KUROPATWA

Biography

JOHN RAYMOND KNISTER was born in Ruscom,[1] near Stoney Point on Lake St. Clair, in Essex County, Ontario, on 27 May 1899. His mother was a teacher, his father a farmer "extremely active in the social and political life of Ontario farmers":[2] what is probably a fictionalized account of this activity is found in Knister's still unpublished novel "Turning Loam." Reading and writing appealed to Knister from the first; he kept a record of his reading between late 1914 and mid-1924 in which over a thousand works are listed,[3] and he started writing as a teenager. There is evidence that much of his poetry was written in the early 1920s,[4] and his first published story, "The One Thing," appeared in the January 1922 issue of the American publication *The Midland*,[5] a magazine that H. L. Mencken described as "perhaps the most important magazine ever founded in America."[6]

In 1919 Knister attended the University of Toronto, until he was hospitalized for pneumonia (Waddington, p. 176). While at the university, he contributed to his college's publication *Acta Victoriana*,[7] and was the student of Pelham Edgar, author of *Henry James, Man and Author* (1927).

From 1920 to 1923 he wrote while working on his father's farm near Blenheim, Ontario. It was during this time that "Mist Green Oats," probably his best-known short story, appeared (O'Halloran, p. 195). By the autumn of 1922, Knister turned his attention to novel writing; he also began reviewing books for a Windsor newspaper, *The Border Cities Star*, and "within a year earned for the *Star* the reputation of printing one of Canada's outstanding Literary Pages" (Waddington, p. 179).

In the autumn of 1923 Knister moved to Iowa City:

Knister began his work with *The Midland* in October, 1923 as the Associate Editor. This was a special new position representing a kind of scholarship Frederick [the editor] had created for young writers of exceptional promise. Ruth Suckow had been the first appointed to the position a year before. Knister's duties ranged through almost every aspect of *Midland* work, and included reading and judging manuscripts, proofreading them and participating in editorial decisions. He was entitled to choose his own hours, perhaps two or three a day, so as to have substantial leisure for his own creative work. (Waddington, p. 179)

Knister attended courses at Iowa University and completed two still unpublished novels, "Group Portrait" and "Turning Loam," while working on *The Midland*.[8] After his term as associate editor ended in June 1924, he went to Chicago, where he wrote during the day and drove taxi by night. Chicago would become the setting for more than one work: the short story "Hackman's Night," the published novella "Innocent Man," and the unpublished novella "Cab Driver" (which surfaced only in January 1984). In October 1924 Knister left Chicago to return to Canada; this homecoming is considered to be the background to the poem "After Exile" (Waddington, p. 181).

By 1925 his work appeared in *This Quarter*, an American expatriate magazine published in Paris, in which the work of Djuna Barnes, E. E. Cummings, Ernest Hemingway, James Joyce, and Carl Sandburg also appeared (Waddington, p. 182). In a letter from Ernest Walsh, editor of *This Quarter*, Knister was told, "Your stuff is real."[9]

Knister wrote many reviews, articles, and sketches for popular magazines and newspapers, but a 1925 letter suggests that he tolerated rather than rejoiced in bread-and-butter composition:

You will be interested to know that I have taken on the job of turning out a story a week . . . a series of rural character sketches — *Toronto Star Weekly*'s request . . . . Loth to have anything to do with Can. (or any other kind of) journalism, I says, How much? 2 c. per word, quoth 'e. Aweel, says I, you've brought it on yourself.[10]

In 1926 Knister moved to Toronto, where he wrote full-time. It was during his years in Toronto that he met Morley Callaghan,

Dorothy Livesay, Wilson MacDonald, Charles G. D. Roberts, Mazo de la Roche, and Duncan Campbell Scott. It was also during the Toronto years that he became the mentor of Thomas Murtha, whose short stories were not published in book form until 1980.[11]

Knister married Myrtle Gamble in 1927, and the couple spent the summer at the "Poplars," a cottage at Hanlan's Point, Toronto Island. Here Knister completed the final draft of *White Narcissus*, his only novel to be published during his lifetime. In September 1927, Macmillan accepted the novel for publication and in October commissioned him to edit an anthology of Canadian short stories (Waddington, p. 186). *Canadian Short Stories*, dedicated to Duncan Campbell Scott, was published in 1928 and is thought to be the first anthology of its kind. Knister's Introduction to the collection is still considered a helpful discussion of the Canadian short story. In 1929 *White Narcissus* was published in Canada, England, and the United States.

In the spring of 1929 Knister and his wife moved to a farmhouse on the lake road near Port Dover, Ontario; here he wrote *My Star Predominant*, a well-researched novel based on the life of John Keats. A daughter, Imogen, was born in Port Dover in 1930. *Show Me Death*, a World War I novel, appeared in 1930 under the name of W. Redvers Dent, but was actually, to a currently unknown extent, ghost-written by Knister. Frederick Philip Grove encouraged Knister to submit *My Star Predominant* to the Graphic Publishers' Canadian Novel Contest; Grove was chairman of the committee adjudicating the award, the other committee members being W. T. Allison, who taught English at the University of Manitoba, and Barker Fairley, who taught German at the University of Toronto.[12] The novel won the $2,500 first prize in 1931, but Graphic went bankrupt and the novel did not appear until 1934, when it was published in Canada and England. Knister had written *My Star Predominant* between 1929 and 1931; the dates of composition of other works overlap with the time of writing the novel: "Innocent Man" was written between 1927 and 1931, while "Cab Driver" was written between 1927 and 1930.[13]

In 1931 and 1932 Knister lived in Quebec, first in Montreal and then in Ste. Anne de Bellevue: it was while in Quebec that his friendship with Leo Kennedy was established.[14] Knister's last novel, "Soil in Smoke," was written between 1931 and 1932; it is a revised version of his first novel, "Group Portrait."[15] Both remain unpublished. During the same period, Knister wrote a number of short stories and the novella "Peaches, Peaches" (O'Halloran, p. 198). He returned to Ontario in 1932 and was offered a job on the editorial staff of Ryerson Press that would allow him time for his own writing.

Raymond Knister drowned while swimming off Stoney Point, Lake St. Clair, on 29 August 1932. An account of this last day has been published.[16] He was thirty-three at the time of his death.

Knister was a writer of short stories, novellas, and novels, as well as being a poet, critic, editor, and playwright. Much of his writing remains unpublished, and therefore unknown. However, during the 1970s some works were published for the first time, and some reprinted, and with this revival of interest emerged a reevaluation of his role in Canadian letters as being that of an interesting but minor author. An important contribution to this reevaluation is the Knister issue of the *Journal of Canadian Fiction* (1975), also published in book form as *Raymond Knister: Poems, Stories and Essays*, in which work by and about Knister appears.

The first selection of Knister's poetry to appear in book form was edited by Dorothy Livesay and published as *Collected Poems of Raymond Knister* (1949). Further poems, many previously unpublished, appear in *Raymond Knister: Poems, Stories and Essays* and *Windfalls for Cider: The Poems of Raymond Knister* (1983). There is no collected edition of Knister's short stories, but many can be found in *Selected Stories of Raymond Knister* (1972), *Raymond Knister: Poems, Stories and Essays*, and *The First Day of Spring: Stories and Other Prose* (1976). Of Knister's nine currently known works of longer prose fiction, five remain unpublished.

Tradition and Milieu

It is difficult to associate Knister's work strictly with any single literary tradition and maintain an accurate sense of his work as a whole. Knister has usually been described as working within the tradition of literary realism, but the complexity and range of his writing suggest that his work should receive more careful attention than it has in the past. In his own critical writing there is cross-reference between forms: for example, he observes that the short story has an "adaptability to poetical interpretation";[17] elsewhere, that Edwin Arlington Robinson is "the Conrad of the narrative poem," as Browning "had been its Henry James."[18] Furthermore, Knister read widely, tended to be experimental, valued the artist who had the courage to express his personal vision, and felt the appeal of the eclectic. He considered himself a Canadian writer and saw Canada as a place where "we have room for all schools, space to be free of all schools."[19] But his view was not isolationist: "Criticism on the part of readers, yes, by all means. But not the kind which assumes that a book is going to be good or bad because it is Canadian."[20]

Yeats remarked that after "established things were shaken by the Great War," there arose the feeling that

> poetry must resemble prose, and both must accept the vocabulary of their time; nor must there be any special subject-matter. Tristram and Isoult were not a more suitable theme than Paddington Railway Station.[21]

Knister's work exhibits the thematic range that Yeats speaks of: the "ill-starred lovers of romance, Tristram and Isoult," are mentioned in *White Narcissus*,[22] and in the Foreword intended for "Windfalls for Cider," a proposed selection of his poems, Knister writes, "Birds and flowers and dreams are real as sweating men and swilling pigs."[23] Knister did not divorce theory from practice; if he is usually remembered for his observant and evocative nature poetry, he is also the author of prose fiction depicting acute psychological tension, imprisonment, racial hostility, and sexual politics.

Knister describes the Canadian writers "Scott, Roberts, Carman, E. W. Thomson, W. W. Campbell, and Lampman" as having to work in a situation in which " . . . the normal response of a writer to his environment was that of a more or less thoroughly transplanted Englishman."[24] He adds that the Canadian poet sometimes

> did not even keep his eye accurately upon the object, and too often he lapsed into a weak-kneed banality of line and a dependence upon the quality of recognition in his reader. "That is good verse, it reminds me of Shelley." It is not to be supposed that a poet of Lampman's gifts would now begin a sonnet, "Beautiful are thy hills, Wayagamack" . . . . (p. 457)

In an article summing up the state of Canadian poetry, published in 1928, Knister speaks of the Canadian poets he prefers:

There was an exquisite Spartan humanity in Isabel Valency Crawford. Archibald Lampman made objective nature pictures as delicate and firm as those of any literature . . . . Charles G. D. Roberts . . . evoked a varied experience with fine insight, and a faith in life itself rare in Canadian poetry . . . . Duncan Campbell Scott seems to have been the surest artist in dealing with a variety of subject matter; he shows unusual restraint of emotion and a fine sense of words.[25]

The Imagist movement has been considered the greatest single influence on Knister's poetry. Knister's evaluation of the importance of the technical aspects of writing reflects Imagist concerns. In his "Credo," Pound writes, "I think . . . that some poems may have form as a tree has form, some as water poured into a vase" and refers to "technique of surface and technique of content."[26] Knister observes,

> Now technique is not merely an exterior matter; or even if it be that it is as the bark of a tree is exterior — and essential. Your subject will be changed, added to, weakened, heightened, or diminished, by a change of method.[27]

A comment of Knister's (made in the course of his essay on Lampman's poetry) has been described by Livesay as a statement of his aesthetic: " 'Poetry is to make things real — those of the imagination,' and those of the tangible world.' "[28] Elsewhere Knister writes, " . . . poetry must have, or rather has a connection with life" ("Canadian Letter," p. 381). And, again in his essay on Lampman, he defines the "basic and enduring qualities" of poetry as being "truth of thought, integrity of feeling, and tempered expression" (pp. 457–58).

Marcus Waddington points out that Knister, like Poe, thought in terms of some continuity between poetry and the short story (Waddington, Thesis, p. 20). Knister refers to one of his short stories (likely "The Strawstack") as being "obviously derived from Poe" ("Canadian Literati," p. 166), and he writes of the short story as "the ark and covenant of Maupassant, Tchekov and Poe" ("Democracy and the Short Story," p. 146). But it is Chekhov who is seen as the master: " . . . since he is to the short story what Shakespeare is to the poetic drama, the form can never be quite the same again."[29] Waddington calls this "symbolic form" and describes Knister's short stories as influenced by Chekhov's technique:

It involves the art of infusing a story with an inner radiance by virtue of which every word, every object and action, every aspect of character, situation and landscape reflects upon and reveals the significance of every other. (Waddington, Thesis, p. 31)

Knister notes that the "modern novelist" has "concerns deriving from James and Flaubert,"[30] and that " . . . it is his view of the world which the artist seeks to impart as Henry James has said."[31] In his Introduction to *Canadian Short Stories*, Knister states:

When Flaubert is bringing some undeniable picture to your recognition, he is doing it only to impose upon you some emotion which is part of his plan and the outgrowth of his own emotion. What is known as realism is only a means to an end, the end being a personal projection of the world.[32]

James refers to Flaubert in the same preface in which he defines his understanding of the literary label "romance,"[33] a definition generally helpful in considering the work of American nineteenth-century writers of romance.[34] Knister refers to James, Melville, and Poe in his critical work, and in *White Narcissus*, as the crisis of the novel nears, the protagonist reaches for Hawthorne's *The Scarlet Letter*.[35] In Knister's remark that the best "American short story writers . . . care more for emotional authenticity than for ingenuity of plot, or for too explicit realism" ("Democracy and the Short Story," p. 148), perhaps there is some empathy with Hawthorne's observation that the writer of romance ought not "swerve aside from the truth of the human heart."[36]

Certainly Knister had little use for the type of romance that celebrates "times when gentlemen carried swords and yearned to use them, if possible on pretext of a lady's honour."[37] He was interested in the possibilities of literary realism, although he refers to going "beyond realism"[38] as moving in a positive direction. "Perhaps," speculates Knister,

it is because of the difficulties attending upon the discovery of the interesting and the heroic in everyday reality that our novelists have tended to shirk the task . . . . [39]

If Knister's view of realism was highly positive, it was not un-qualified: "Realism is not . . . to be accepted as an end in itself, nor, at its best, as an unmixed good, but as bringing a depth of knowledge and conviction and authenticity of feeling together with a more revealing portrayal of our inner life."[40] Although Knister employs the techniques of literary realism, his work can be viewed as open to the influence of more than one tradition.

Knister expresses a definite aversion to an author distrusting, misrepresenting, or violating "experienced reality" ("The Poetry of Archibald Lampman," p. 458): characters in fiction, he writes, "may transcend the people we see about us, but they must be true to them, and true to type."[41] He rejects the attitude that caused the editor of the *Toronto Star Weekly* to "expostulate earnestly . . . 'Mr. Knister, you make your people too real. Our readers don't want to read about real things. They want to be amused. Try to put more plot into your stories' " ("Canadian Literati," p. 164). Knister had little patience for any "yea-saying protagonist of all's-wellness."[42] Despite the fact that he "was sure that there were some thousands of readers of the paper who would like to see their life pictured more or less as it was" ("Canadian Literati," p. 165), such potential readers were, as David Arnason points out, "protested from Knister by conservative editors."[43] In summing up the essay "Canadian Literati," Knister remarks, "I am only pointing out that we probably will have to come to grips with reality before we shall have a literature . . . " (p. 167).

Knister's milieu included many of the Toronto literati of his day (see "Biography" above); correspondents included Harriet Monroe, Pelham Edgar, Frederick Philip Grove, Leo Kennedy, A. J. M. Smith, Thomas Murtha, Morley Callaghan, John T. Frederick, Dorothy Livesay, Duncan Campbell Scott, and Ruth Suckow. Letters between Knister and Murtha, and Knister's correspondence with various publishing houses, provide windows through which to glimpse the literary life of the era. Letters from Grove to Knister have been published,[44] and correspondence with Knister is quoted, and his connection with *Saturday Night* briefly discussed, in a biography of William Arthur Deacon.[45] William Murtha discusses the relationship between Thomas Murtha and Knister in his Introduction to *Short Stories of Thomas Murtha*.[46]

Knister is remembered in various forms of memoir. The dedication of Leo Kennedy's *The Shrouding* reads "For / Raymond Knister

/ one year dead."⁴⁷ A large proportion of *Collected Poems of Raymond Knister* (1949) consists of Dorothy Livesay's memoir, an abridged version of which is reprinted in *Right Hand Left Hand*.⁴⁸ A CBC Radio program about Knister included contributions from Nathaniel Benson, Morley Callaghan, Philip Child, Wilfrid Eggleston, Wilson MacDonald, James Reaney, and Knister's wife.⁴⁹ (For Reaney's assessment of Knister's work, made in this context, see "Critical Overview and Context" below.) In 1976 a memoir by Leo Kennedy appeared,⁵⁰ and meeting Knister at Pelham Edgar's home is recollected in Earle Birney's *Spreading Time*.⁵¹

In "Raymond Knister — Man or Myth?" Imogen Knister Givens discusses her father's life and career, quotes a diary entry of her mother's describing the day of Knister's death, and refutes Livesay's "suicide theory" concerning Knister.⁵² In her "Afterword" to *Windfalls for Cider*, Givens outlines Knister's literary "accomplishments, in which Canadians might take pride" (*WC*, p. 77), notes that "the distorted perception of his personality has led to a misunderstanding of his work," and calls for "a fresh look at his work" (*WC*, p. 80).

Dorothy Livesay, James Reaney, and David Arnason have all pointed to the power of Knister's writing, but most critics have not explored the literary roots of Knister's work to any great extent, and there has been slight discussion of Knister in the context of his cultural era. However, Knister's letters include, for example, references to Lawren Harris and A. Y. Jackson,⁵³ to Emma Goldman,⁵⁴ and to his visiting, while in New York, "Greenwich Village where the artists and writers (used to) hang out."⁵⁵ The totality of Knister's work, too much of which remains unpublished or unreprinted, and the Knister papers and letters suggest that Knister has been overlooked as a major Canadian writer — if not *the* major Canadian writer — of the 1920s.

Critical Overview and Context

Knister's poetry did not appear in book form during his lifetime, although his work was published in avant-garde journals. In 1925 the serial poem "A Row of Horse Stalls" appeared in *This Quarter*, and *The New Criterion*'s review of the issue describes "Raymond Knister's poems" as being "fresh and objective."⁵⁶

Collected Poems of Raymond Knister (1949), which was edited by Dorothy Livesay and was actually a selection of his work, was the first book of Knister's poetry to appear. It includes Livesay's "Raymond Knister: A Memoir," a rather psycho-biographical discussion of his life and career, in which Livesay quotes liberally from Knister's letters and delineates his cultural milieu. Also included in the *Collected Poems* is Knister's Foreword to "Windfalls for Cider." Livesay's decision to publish the Foreword made available for the first time this brief but significant statement, which reflects, as Livesay notes elsewhere, Knister's "aims as a writer."[57] In her memoir, Livesay identifies a central poetic concern of Knister's as being akin to one of Rilke's:

> Knister's object, in writing poetry, was to present the object seen, the thing felt, as simply and feelingly as possible. Rilke's concern for perception, even of the smallest object, was Knister's also, before he had ever heard of Rilke. Nearly ten years later, when he had caught up with contemporary aesthetics, he began shaping his own, and stating it. "Poetry is to make things real — those of the imagination, and those of the tangible world." (p. xxi)

For Livesay, Knister's poems constitute "the best" of "all the legacies Raymond Knister has given Canada" (p. xl).

Some reactions to Livesay's memoir seem to focus at least as much on biographical as on critical material. One review notes that "due tribute" is paid to Knister's "simple, intense, honest way of living, thinking and writing."[58] Another review calls for "more detail, more personal anecdote and more comment."[59] Milton Wilson's 1960 article "Klein's Drowned Poet: Canadian Variations on an Old Theme" opens: "Raymond Knister must be the best-known drowned poet in Canadian letters." Knister, "writer of pastorals and herald of imagism, cut off at the age of thirty-three,"[60] receives almost no further attention other than a brief allusion to the poem Livesay dedicates to him ("The Outrider") and a description of his appearances in James Reaney's 1958 *A Suit of Nettles*. Wilson's article exemplifies how biographical interest in Knister can overwhelm attention to his work.

In his memoir *Spreading Time*, Earle Birney includes, under the heading "About Reaney and Knister," the text of his 1949 radio review of Reaney's *The Red Heart* and the *Collected Poems of*

Raymond Knister. Birney finds Knister to be "an honest objective artist and a pioneer in Canadian realism," whose "poetic technique is largely confined to that kind of rural understatement and casualness which Robert Frost used more richly, or to the rather monotonously-etched free verse of the Imagists."[61] Munro Beattie, in the *Literary History of Canada: Canadian Literature in English*, states that Knister's " 'The Plowman' and 'Ambition' and 'White Cat' have something of the accent of Robert Frost." Knister's poetry is also said to show the influence of William Carlos Williams, the *Spoon River Anthology*, and Imagism. Beattie asserts that Knister "had learned — almost alone among Canadian writers of the twenties — the principal requisite of free verse: that cadence and feeling must be thoroughly fused, as, for instance, in 'The Colt.' "[62]

Peter Stevens' 1965 article "The Old Futility of Art: Knister's Poetry" (the title is from Knister's poem "Moments when I'm Feeling Poems") also refers to the Imagist influence on Knister's poetry. Stevens discusses Knister's treatment of the themes of nature and language. In Knister's discussion of Lampman, Stevens finds "a suggestion that Knister feels in the other poet the sense of a separation between man and nature."[63] "The Colt" is cited as an example of this same separation in Knister's own verse for, Stevens claims, " . . . the farmer's comment at the end of the poem . . . emphasizes the world of difference between man and nature" (p. 47). According to Stevens, in Knister's poetry, "horses often become symbols of the stoic pattern of nature," and they "always show an acceptance of their lives" (p. 47). In "The Plowman" and "Lake Harvest," Stevens sees "the horse's calm acceptance" as "contrasted to man's labour, which often seems so futile in most of Knister's poetry" (pp. 47–48). "Moments when I'm Feeling Poems" reflects, for Stevens, "a conflict between the poet's vision and the inadequacy of language to express that vision. This is the 'old futility of art.' Words always distort the poet's vision . . . " (p. 49). Stevens asks if Knister might "recognize within himself the impossibility of communicating his vision" (p. 49). Thus he implies that Knister's poetry is, at least to some extent, a poetry of perpetual defeat: there is "the barrenness of language, but its final treachery may be that it seems to offer eventual success" (p. 50).

Stevens' view influenced subsequent discussion of Knister's poetry. George A. Ross, in his 1969 M.A. Thesis, "Three Minor Canadian Poets: Louis Alexander MacKay, Leo Kennedy and Raymond Knister," is in essential agreement with the views expressed by Livesay and

Stevens. There is a strong element of the psycho-biographical in Ross's discussion. He finds that the "basic tension between man and his environment is central to all of Knister's poems."[64] Bernhard Beutler's 1978 *Der Einfluss des Imagismus auf die moderne kanadische Lyrik englischer Sprache* includes a discussion of Knister's work under the heading " 'Herald of Imagism': Raymond Knister." Beutler comments, " . . . sein Thema bleibt das bäuerliche Land, seine Methode ist die Beobachtung, seine Darstellung sparsame Dokumentation."[65] There is an echo of Stevens' view of the relationship between man and nature in Knister's poetry in Beutler's statement "Ein Beispiel für Knisters Leitmotiv, des Kampfes mit oder auch gegen die Natur, ist der 'Plowman's Song' " (p. 44). Beutler asserts that Knister refused to be restricted by the terms of systems, categories, or poetic movements, as these would impair choice of content (p. 47).

Don Precosky's 1980 article "Ever with Discontent: Some Comments on Raymond Knister and His Poetry" (the title is from Knister's poem "The Plowman") again notes Knister's debt to the Imagists and the similarity of his work to Robert Frost's. But Precosky states that Knister's work differs from that of the Imagists both in being rural rather than urban and being "less coldly objective" in "tone."[66] Another American influence which Precosky identifies arises from the fact that "Knister served his literary apprenticeship in the American midwest and his poetry, like Sandburg's, was regional and realistic" (p. 4). Knister, writes Precosky, "valued plough horses above winged ones" (p. 4). Precosky disagrees with Stevens' assertion that in Knister's poetry horses "always show an acceptance of their lives," and he cites the last stanza of "Nell" in support of this contention (p. 6). However, his interpretation of "Moments when I'm Feeling Poems" substantially agrees with that of Stevens. "Before he begins Knister knows he will fail," claims Precosky, who goes on to explain, "As I read Knister's poetry, the central theme emerges as man's desire for fulfilment through the accomplishment of perfect action. This action may be ploughing a straight furrow or writing the perfect poem"; but this "quest" for "perfect action" is "doomed from the beginning" (p. 8).

Marcus Waddington's extensively researched 1977 M.A. Thesis, "Raymond Knister and the Canadian Short Story," does not focus on, but briefly discusses, Knister's poetry. Waddington contends that Stevens "fails to realize that Knister was encouraging not the 'separation between man and nature' in Lampman's poetry but rather Lampman's ability to experience reality as an integrated whole. Stevens' interpretation of Knister's approach to the environment is diametrically opposed to Knister's own point of view" (pp. 82–83). "For Knister," writes Waddington, "a writer's treatment of Nature as an object on which he imposed 'his own tempers' was not artistic technique but a vicarious means of escape" (p. 81). Waddington observes that "the tension in Knister's poetry originates in his vision of life as a process of constant change" (p. 83). In considering how Knister works with the subjective and objective, Waddington suggests that "Knister's poems can generally be divided into two different kinds":

> poems in which the environment is observed and the speaker is absent, such as "Snowfall," "Quiet Snow" and "Bees," and poems in which the environment is observed by a speaker who is present, such as "Night Walk," "October Stars," "The Motor: A Fragment" and "Reply to August." The one kind can be . . . termed poems of observation, and the other, poems of involvement.
>
> If we consider the speaker as equivalent to the poet, as Knister does in his essay on Lampman, then the poet is outside the poem in poems of observation and inside the poem in poems of involvement. Yet the mood of the poet makes itself felt in both kinds of poems; while this mood is suggested in poems of observation, it is recorded in poems of involvement. (pp. 84–85)

Waddington's remarks help explain the fine tuning of viewpoint found in Knister's best work.

The question of the role of Knister's poetry in the development of Canadian writing has received some attention. Birney and Wilson, as well as Northrop Frye in his "Conclusion" to the *Literary History of Canada*,[67] all associate the work of Knister with that of James Reaney. Apart from Knister's appearance in *A Suit of Nettles*, Reaney comments, in a CBC Radio profile of Knister, "I think he did something genuinely classical — that means something that's permanent in the poems."[68] As well, Reaney's Preface introduces *Windfalls for Cider*, a 1983 selection of Knister's poetry.

David Arnason's 1975 article "Canadian Poetry: The Interregnum" makes a convincing argument for a reevaluation of Canadian poets writing between the wars: Louise Morey Bowman, Lawren Harris, W. W. E. Ross, and Raymond Knister. Arnason describes Knister as "perhaps the chief Canadian talent of the twenties" (p. 31). He characterizes his poetry as "realistic, in the sense that its main aim is to capture the world of sense experience. The poems Knister writes are richly sensuous and evocative, though their form is starkly simple" (p. 31). For example, " . . . 'In the Rain, Sowing Oats' provides a simple but highly textured image" (p. 31), while "The Hawk," with its combination of "sharp, simple images, rich, evocative diction, and smooth, inevitable language" can, as "descriptive poetry," "stand with anything written by any poet in the twentieth Rcentury, whatever his country" (p. 32).

Arnason points the way for future discussion of Knister's poetry when he comments that "Knister did not limit himself to simple descriptive and imagist poems." He continues:

> The ten poems that make up "A Row of Stalls" are each individual descriptions of farm horses; and each, in spite of the unlikeliness of the subject matter is successful. Taken together, they evoke a broader society, both equine and human, filled with love, death, hate, terror and pride, and they conjure up a world of work and aristocratic pleasure inhabited by Teddy Roosevelt, Sarah Bernhard and Henry Ford.
>
> "Poisons" is as modern in its concerns as it is in its prose-poem form. (p. 32)

Arnason's discussion raises issues that have not received sufficient critical attention. The World War I veteran who, in "Poisons," remembers gas warfare in Europe as he sprays a peach orchard with chemicals is in many ways a far more typical Knister figure than most critics would allow. In general, Knister's writing is marked by a recurrent interest in presenting man in terms of his social and physical environment, so that there is identification, rather than isolation, of individual concerns. The range and themes of Knister's poetry deserve further exploration.

Knister's Works

The vision of reality which informs Raymond Knister's writing is one which celebrates the acknowledgement of experience; in

Knister's own words, "Reality is fine in spite of its grossness and cruelty."[69] Critics identify this impulse underlying Knister's work in different formulations: Livesay states that in his work Knister "was able to make the ordinary extraordinary";[70] in "Canadian Poetry: The Interregnum," Arnason writes that Knister's "poems, stories and novels all reveal his excited awareness that the ordinary things around him really mattered" (p. 31); and in his Preface to *Windfalls for Cider*, Reaney notes that Knister's poetry can imply that " . . . your life is potentially more interesting than you ever thought possible" (*WC*, p. 7). Knister's poetry, like his prose fiction, explores realities both tangible and intangible; while in his best poetry there is an application of his belief that to have "the courage of our experience" (Foreword, in *WC*, p. 15) is to have a sound basis for art.

Knister is probably as provocative a critic as he is evocative a poet. For him, poetry is neither a tidy refuge nor a trivial pursuit:

In view of the fact that the people who think that Canadian poetry is not important usually have read or tried to read some of it, an estimate should be made of what Canadian poets have done and not done; but still more urgently needed is a summation, here too brief, of the nature of poetry. This seems to be very poorly understood, owing largely to the teaching in schools. Poetry, as the growing boy conceives it, is a series of lines each beginning with a capital letter, sometimes indented, and rhymed more or less regularly at the end. The words make a kind of jingle in your ear, sometimes pleasing, but usually so silly as to subject matter that the greatest inducements can scarcely make you commit it to memory. Whatever it is written about is so remote from life that it is impossible to imagine that it could have any meaning that mattered . . . . What people don't see or forget is that in so far as they are living they are living poetry. An amusing instance of such obtuseness was an article in this journal some months ago by someone, presumably a business man not writing with his tongue in his cheek, who condemned poetry as a total loss, and claimed in effect that no line of poetry was worth a good dinner.

This man did not see that even a good dinner is impossible in its fullest flowering without poetry. The good dinner may seem only a matter of material victuals and corporeal digestive capabilities. But in our day the good dinner will not mean much unless its appeal to the palate arouses desire, emotion, and unless the *idea* of a good dinner means something beautiful. In fact if dinners were postponed from year to year, I have no doubt that poetry as passionate would be written about them as has been written to girls by love-lorn swains in these last centuries of romance. ("The Poetic Muse in Canada," p. 3)

The key phrase here is "remote from life," a phrase which defines quite accurately what Knister's work generally avoids. Knister's poetry evokes the appeal of things and moments that are part of everyday life; his writing reflects the reality of the material world, as well as psychological truths and realities the imagination generates or elucidates.

The poem "White Cat" (WC, p. 21) illustrates how Knister's poetry can blend attention to different but continuous aspects of reality. Simplicity marks the poem's opening line: "I like to go to the stable after supper." The second line, "Remembering fried potatoes and tarts of snow-apple jam," belies the simplicity of the opening line by evoking memory, sensory perception, and highly specific, and local, detail. The boy who is the narrator of the poem refers to a "White Cat" that crosses his path as he and his father return, "with the milk," from the stable to the house. Knister leaves precisely what the "White Cat" stands for open to question. The White Cat may be an ordinary pet seen with the intensity of unfettered or unjaded imagination, be a figment of the boy's active imagination, symbolize imagination itself, or even represent a combination of possible meanings. In Knister's poem, whatever the White Cat itself may mean, there is a discoverable excitement to everyday life. The power of the boy's imagination enables him to perceive magic in the so-called ordinary; Knister suggests that the magic stems from everyday life — it is not antithetical to it.

As "White Cat" moves from tangible to intangible realities, one apparently moves from material reality to arrive at the reality of the imagination, but the importance of this imaginative world is that it stems from the actual world, and finally reflects back upon it. At work is a principle of attachment, rather than detachment; as Knister writes in another context, " . . . poetry must have, or rather has a connection with life . . . " ("Canadian Letter," p. 381). When Knister denies the value of poetry that would be "remote from life," he presumably does not mean that the poet is to restrict himself to flat, literal depiction. The White Cat that the imagination perceives is as real as a plain white cat. Where the lie presumably sets in is in detachment from life, in the impulse to cleave poetry from life, and in the attempt to disconnect the imaginative from the actual. Knister's position on the nature of poetry is continuous with the recurrent presentation, in his poetry and prose fiction, of consciousness in relation to environment, rather than isolated from it. His writing generally balances what one sees with how one envisions the world, so that what becomes acknowledged is, as he writes in the poem "After Exile,"

> Like the water-mark in this paper,
> There if you like, or if you forget,
> Not there.
>
> (WC, p. 47)

Knister evokes the barely visible water-mark of the page as he does the White Cat that the imagination makes of a plain pet: the poet takes realities of various degrees of tangibility and positions them within the range of visibility or intelligibility. The formal simplicity of some of Knister's poems does not preclude sophistication. As "White Cat" exemplifies, Knister is able to use simple language to create complex resonances. "Plowman's Song" is perhaps deceptively simple in form:

> Turn under, plow,
> My trouble;
> Turn under griefs
> And stubble.
>
> Turn mouse's nest,
> Gnawing years;
> Old roots up
> For new love's tears.
>
> Turn plow, the clods
> For new thunder.
> Turn under, plow,
> Turn under.
>
> (WC, p. 46)

The shape of "Plowman's Song" is slender, the lines brief; the pared down, spare form matches the simplicity of the language used. But because, in contrast, the resonances created are complex, the effect achieved is one of great concentration. Knister coordinates the tension between the contained and the continuous. The shape of the poem, and the simplicity of its language, give the impression of the self-contained, an impression strengthened by the poem opening and closing with the same phrase, but within this highly contained structure Knister evokes the uncontainable workings of consciousness.

Over the course of the poem, the plowman's thoughts and action are successively paired, blended with increasing intensification, and finally seen in synthesis; the phrase "new thunder" refers to both the plowman's worlds of reverie and work. But such containment is a synthesis or sum that is greater than its constituent parts. The first verse of "Plowman's Song" refers to individual concern, the second speaks of the individual in relationship with another, if not in idyllic relationship, and in the third verse the concern with work, which runs throughout, becomes blended with the subjects of the plowman's reverie. The contemplative life and active life of the plowman are ultimately continuous, and the implication is that there is a continuity not only between man's mental and physical life, but also between man and his environment. The fluidity of consciousness, as well as the continuity that exists between man and his environment, are held in tension with the sense of containment or confinement that the form and diction of the poem suggest.

In "Plowman's Song," the treatment of subject matter points outward, to the uncontainable nature of consciousness. Within this overall pattern, there is an impulse towards the discovery of harmonies, rather than oppositions. Instead of the opposition of a fixed pattern of work to the fluidity of consciousness, there is a blending of these two aspects of existence. The presented patterns of thought are not chained to the patterns of work, but rather the rhythms of one harmoniously follow the rhythms of the other. It is the harmonious existence of the two that counts.

"The Plowman" also presents consciousness in relation to environment, although the relationship presented is a more problematical one than that found in "Plowman's Song":

All day I follow
Watching the swift dark furrow

That curls away before me,
And care not for skies or upturned flowers,
And at the end of the field
Look backward
Ever with discontent.
A stone, a root, a strayed thought
Has warped the line of that furrow —
And urge my horses 'round again.

Sometimes even before the row is finished
I must look backward;
To find, when I come to the end
That there I swerved.

Unappeased I leave the field,
Expectant, return.

The horses are very patient.
When I tell myself
This time
The ultimate unflawed turning
Is before my share,
They must give up their rest.

(WC, p. 20)

The first verse of "The Plowman" is the longest of the poem, being almost as long as the other verses put together; in formal terms, Knister calls particular attention to the first verse, giving it the most weight. What the first verse establishes is a misconception held by the plowman. He directs his attention almost exclusively to the job at hand, and while he recognizes that something is amiss, he does not seem to be consciously aware that it might have some relation to his oblivion towards "skies or upturned flowers," although there is a suggestion that he might be making such a connection at a sub-conscious level. When the plowman considers "A stone, a root, a strayed thought" in series, he effectively groups them together, and in doing so gives tacit, if unconscious, recognition to the ecological continuity that characterizes the natural world and includes man.

Such recognition is still only at the threshold of his conscious-ness; the plowman groups together representatives of the mineral, vegetable, and human worlds in the first verse of the poem only in order to identify the cause of the "warped line" of his furrow. His concern with the undeviatingly linear, his strict attention to his work, differentiates him from the plowman in "Plowman's Song," who is associated with a recognition of curvilinearity, who does not allow his consciousness to be chained to the patterns of his work, and whose song acknowledges the continuity between the worlds of man and nature. The difference between the plowman of "Plowman's Song" and the obsessive figure with which "The Plowman" opens is analagous to the difference between character types described in another Knister poem, "The Motor: A Fragment," in which one can drive

> Past farms quiet and busy and sane, with weedy fronts,
> Past homes of the idler, and the man who would kill himself
> With the pride of his work,
> That have no weeds along the road.

(WC, p. 59)

Obsession similarly rules negative characters in Knister's fiction. As the title of the short story "The One Thing" hints, an obsessive, single interest is of central importance; the protagonist's preoccupation with "one thing," in combination with his isolation, eventually destroys him. In the novel *White Narcissus*, obsessed characters create problems for others, and this is presumably why *White Narcissus* includes overt reference to Nathaniel Hawthorne's great study of obsession, *The Scarlet Letter*.[71]

In the second verse of "The Plowman," the plowman's very attitude of fixed attention to his work is beginning to disrupt it. However, there is a suggestion of the gradual erosion of his initial outlook. In the first verse, his attitude is such that he describes departure from a straight furrow as "warped," but the word he uses in the second verse to describe the same thing is "swerved," a less severe term. The plowman's initial alienation from the natural world, earlier expressed in his desire to impose a rigid "line" on the land, gradually decreases.

In the third verse of the poem, movement in space reflects a shift of psychological position. The "unappeased" plowman of the first verse leaves the field in the third verse, and at this point metaphorically departs from his previous position as well. An "expectant" plowman returns to the field, rather than one rife with "discontent." The fourth and final verse suggests why the plowman leaves his discontent behind.

The final verse's opening line is the only initial line of a verse in the poem that does not refer, or introduce a reference, to the plowman himself. For the first time in the poem, the plowman explicitly avoids seeing himself in the isolated position of mastering the world in which he works. He now sees the horses as "very patient," or sees them as being more than merely instruments of his will. In the second verse, the plowman comments, "I must look backward"; in the fourth verse, that the horses "must give up their rest." By the final verse, then, the plowman can acknowledge that fellow creatures are also subject to dictates. As elsewhere in Knister's work, the attitude exhibited towards horses mirrors character; in the short story "The Loading," a character associated with the maltreatment of horses is also associated with manslaughter.

By the fourth verse, the "line" the plowman sought in the first verse has become "the ultimate unflawed turning" that his "very patient" horses will "give up their rest" for. The use of the word "ultimate" implies that it may not be a strictly agricultural "unflawed turning" that the plowman seeks. What this desire of the plowman's might be remains undefined; Knister leaves this open-ended, as he does the metaphorical meaning of the White Cat. In Hawthorne's work there is more than one way of interpreting a scarlet letter; in Knister's work there is more than one way of seeing a white cat, a white narcissus, or, in the case of "The Plowman," conceiving of purity of "line."

The use of the word "turning" in the final verse of "The Plowman" is a reminder of the prominence of the word "turn," and the implications it carries, in "Plowman's Song." The consciousness of the plowman in "Plowman's Song" seems akin to the consciousness that the figure in "The Plowman" arrives at. The final verse of each poem looks towards the future. It would appear that both plowmen, who acknowledge continuity between the worlds of man and nature, are assigned a future to look forward to.

As mentioned above, David Arnason points out that the "ecological concern" in Knister's poem "Poisons" (WC, p. 50) is "particularly modern," and this observation identifies the sensibility that repeatedly informs both Knister's poetry and prose. In his essay "The Lost Gentleman," Knister asserts that one can trace back to the time "when the doctrine of Darwin had become ingrained in the mentality of the educated" the realization — "with a certainty far beyond sentimental religiosity" — of "the continuity of life, the solidarity of man with 'creeping things' " (p. 151). (While the tone

Knister uses here, in referring to the "educated" and "sentimental religiosity" is perhaps atypical, it should be remembered that Knister's years are 1899–1932, the Scopes monkey trial was in 1925, and Clarence Darrow is mentioned in Knister's work, in the novella "Innocent Man.") For Knister, the "solidarity of man with 'creeping things' " had literary implications. In the 1926 article "Purposes of Fiction," he writes,

> . . . when Conrad scrutinized human character in its various national and individual characteristics, he did so with the greatest care . . . in the interests of truth for the creation of beauty.
>
> Through forms of beauty to share his sense of mystery, terror, delight or ugliness with his fellow-creatures, was the aim which Conrad confessed, which he gave as the aim of the artist in all times and all mediums. To make you see, to make you feel, and to realize the solidarity of all created things under the sun.[72]

One way in which Knister's poetry communicates a sense of ecological continuity is in the use of anthropomorphism. For example, in "Sumach," a "sumach bush" "smiles" and "pretends to sneeze" (WC, p. 25). "Barns four-square in dejection" appear in "Autumn" (WC, p. 57), the moon is "petulant" in "Spring-Flooded Ditches" (WC, p. 43), and ". . . ghost-trees / . . . do not forget / Hot stormlight / Muffling stars" in "Whip-Poor-Will in North Woods" (WC, p. 41). In "Change," "the trees stand tense and lonely" (WC, p. 33), while in "Dog and Cat" (WC, p. 35) domestic animals engage in an anthropomorphized courtship ritual. There are also more subtle acknowledgements of ecological continuity in Knister's poetry. Some poems having "nature" titles and subject matter refer to what could be described as existential anxiety: in "Cedars," human "shoutings" attempt " . . . to shatter / The mist and the frost of the void" (WC, p. 37), while in "Elm Tree and Sun" (WC, p. 43) there is a final reference to "the void" that lies beyond what is familiar.

Even in a descriptive poem like "The Hawk," Knister recognizes ecological relationships in balancing the role of the observed with the role of the observer:

> Across the bristled and sallow fields,
> The speckled stubble of cut clover,
> Wades your shadow.

Or against a grimy and tattered
Sky
You plunge.

Or you shear a swath
From trembling tiny forests
With the steel of your wings —

Or make a row of waves
By the heat of your flight
Along the soundless horizon.

(WC, p. 21)

In every verse, "your" and/or "you" appears, so that there are continual reminders of the presence of an observer. The hawk first appears above "fields," next against the "sky," then near "forests," and finally flies away "along the soundless horizon": the poem describes the bird's flight pattern in terms of the observer's larger sense of the natural world. The hawk is the focus of the observer's attention, but the natural setting also receives attention, and this serves as a reminder that what Knister describes is what his observer perceives. The reader gets the observer's version of the hawk's flight. Knister both gives a description of a hawk and implies that what literature presents as "nature" is subjective, or a matter related to vision. At the same time, the observer's implicit appreciation of the hawk he watches accords with Knister's expressed sense of ecological continuities. As a poet, Knister has less concern with photographing nature than "enimaging" (WC, p. 52) or envisioning it.

Critics repeatedly point to the influence of Imagism in Knister's poetry. While Knister does not deny that Imagism has something to offer, he does maintain that its formulation is restrictive:

This is a comparatively new conception of poetry. It is perhaps a dozen or fifteen years ago that a small band of poets, some American and some English, adopted imagism, in part borrowed from the French, as a creed. This is not expressing it too strongly. The creed was precisely and definitely formulated. Nowadays all poets agree that these rules regarding the use of the exact word, the keeping of the eye on the object, and so forth, are a part of all good writing, prose and verse. But as for making the image the whole poem, that is not accepted by anyone, though many fine poems resulted from such usage.

The idea was, roughly, that each poem should comprise an image, and that this image should not be blurred by extraneous matter. You should not say that this or that was like the other; that was evading the whole issue. You were somehow to convey the identity of your bird or rock or flower or person without comparing it to something else, and without moralizing or generalizing about it.

Undoubtedly this makes for clearer and more objective, chaster art. But it is more limiting than ever the sonnet was. If each poem is to be a single image, it may be perfectly satisfying as such, and yet in many cases fail to move the reader.[73]

What Knister finds of value in Imagism is the uncluttered form it advises. However, he makes it clear that prescriptive technical considerations are not primary — it is not enough if an Imagist poem succeeds according to the Imagist "creed" but fails "to move the reader." He states that poetry is "as much poetry whether it is printed as prose or not" ("On Reading Aloud," p. 14).

In his Foreword to "Windfalls for Cider," Knister seems to suggest that form is a subordinate consideration to the vision with which the artist informs his works. He writes, "In the end we in Canada here might have the courage of our experience and speak according to it only. And when we trust surely, see directly enough, life, ourselves, we may have our own Falstaffs and Shropshire Lads and Anna Kareninas" (WC, p. 15). For Knister, unforgettable figures are of equal importance whether discovered in drama, poetry, or the novel — he exhibits less interest in the form of literature than in what the form expresses.

It has been argued that Knister hints at the self-defeating nature of poetry in "Moments When I'm Feeling Poems," although such an interpretation seems open to debate. The poem reads:

Moments when I'm feeling poems —
Before the stir and clash of words —
When some forgotten clear slight
Secret's imminent plangent chords

Come like a full moon's·night
That has been stolen by rain,
Dimmed grey, radiant but palled —
Moments when beauty creeps like pain,

I know the old futility of art,
But know as well the ladies and the lords
Of life are they who, knowing, feel
No call to blight that sense with words.

(WC, p. 40)

The poem opens by focusing on the time that leads to the writing of poetry, rather than the actual writing of poetry itself. Obscurity marks this stage of composition. The use of the word "moments" in the last line of the second verse indicates that it is still the prearticulation stage of writing poetry that is being evoked. For the poet "beauty creeps like pain," possibly because what the poem is to express still resists articulation. The poem ends with a double recognition on the part of the poet: he knows "the old futility of art"; but he also knows that the " . . . ladies and the lords / Of life . . . ," although "knowing," do not feel obligated to "blight that sense with words." If these recognitions are to be contrasted, and the way they are presented in context encourages such comparison, it is likely that the poet's pronouncement about art is a better index of what is to be upheld than the attitude of the lords and ladies. Their unwillingness to articulate, their obliviousness to the question, is something that clearly runs counter to the sensibility of the poet who takes the trouble to evoke the very process whereby the felt poem is translated into a written work. The poet or the artist is the one who can "know"; the lords and ladies are "knowing," perhaps smugly, imperturbably "knowing."

"Moments When I'm Feeling Poems" can be read as a celebration of the artist's struggle for articulation, the fight to transpose conception into effective execution. In context, the poet/artist's knowledge of "the old futility of art" stands in opposition to ("But know as well") his knowledge of the "knowing," inarticulate lords and ladies of life. As Knister comments in "Canadian Literati," "It is not possible to know too much, but it is easy to know enough to have prejudices and opinions which may warp creation" (p. 167). The artist's struggle for expression is a phase, which will presumably pass, as will the conditions that temporarily dim the radiance of "a full moon's night"; however, the ladies and lords of silent persuasion are associated with "blight," or disease. Knister's poem distinguishes the artist, who persists until the expression he seeks emerges from obscurity, from those who consider the impulse to articulate a "blight," which the *Oxford English Dictionary* defines as "any obscure malignant influence." Perhaps "the old futility of art" is an expression of the artist's protest against the dismissal of art, rather than an indication of a radical discontent with the artistic process or objection to the inadequacy of verbal expression.

The above reading of "Moments When I'm Feeling Poems" is possible strictly in terms of the poem itself; but because the poem has been given another, radically different reading, it might be added that the views Knister expresses elsewhere in his work would make it more probable that he would object to a low regard for art than either the artistic process or the nature of art itself. In his essay "Canadian Literature: A General Impression," Knister observes that " . . . art, and particularly literary art, . . . has the property, not only of revealing, but of forming civilizations" (pp. 171–72). He concludes the essay by defining the "function" of literature as being to "give voice to a deepened consciousness and a broadened civilization" (p. 174). Knister sees artists as "the hope of whatever civilization we are to have above materialism."[74] There is as well some indication that such terms as "lords" and "ladies" do not necessarily carry positive connotations for Knister. The "strolling player," writes Knister, would be in his day considered "at best an intellectual valet to whom the count and the baron could unburden their minds as they could not to their more materialistic equals" ("The Lost Gentleman," p. 150). "Moments When I'm Feeling Poems" can be read as a questioning of the intellectual chastity of those who are chronically inarticulate, and a celebration of the artist who struggles to express his vision.

Knister does not restrict himself to the natural environment as setting or subject in his poetry — there are poems in which there is at least as much concentration on the social world as the natural world. The individual poems that compose "A Row of Stalls" are concise but evocative, and, as David Arnason explains, their total effect is to "evoke a broader society, both equine and human" ("Canadian Poetry: The Interregnum," p. 32). These two worlds serve as double mirrors, which reflect back upon each other. For example, in

"Mack" (WC, p. 27), the horse is man's laughing-stock, but in "Nance" the opposite is the case:

> "She kicked her foot through the dashboard,
> And I made her go, for about a mile."
> The old cattle-dealer's booming voice,
> Like that,
> Must have lent speed to her three legs.
> Then when they got home
> He carefully unharnessed her,
> Clutched her bridle in one hand,
> Half a rail in the other,
> And the dance began.
>
> When Art Huffer got Nance,
> He declared that he would cure her.
> He took ten bushels of corncobs
> Into the loft above her stall;
> All the rainy day he dropped cobs
> And as each one struck her
> She kicked as high as ever:
> Art had to give up too.

(WC, p. 30)

The horses in "A Row of Stalls" are described in terms of character and individual history. In giving this sort of recognition — and in serial amplification — Knister again implies that there is a continuity between the worlds of man and nature. As well, in using this form to conjure up varying aspects of human personality and society — one of the horses, for example, has "fierce ears" and an accompanying "Roosevelt-Wilson-Fairbanks smile" (WC, p. 27) — Knister moves towards writing a twentieth-century animal fable. "Omens of *Animal Farm*" were detected by Peter Stevens in Knister's prose work "A Row of Horse Stalls."[75] The serial poem of the same title was published in 1925, exactly twenty years before Orwell's *Animal Farm*. Although Knister's poem is not characterized by Orwell's ongoing correspondences, it may be described as a work on the road leading towards *Animal Farm*. Knister's prose work "Boquet and Some Buds: A Stable Anthology" also has elements (if to a lesser degree) which would inform *Animal Farm* two decades later:

Her name was Boquet. At first it would seem absurd that a
creature weighing nineteen hundred pounds, however grace-
fully and easily she moved them about, should rejoice in the
name of Boquet. A more than sizable *boutoniere*, somebody
said. Yet her character deserved the name. Always willing,
never laggard, never ill-tempered even when her team-mate
was misbehaving and drawing the wrath of the driver upon
both their heads, her character was ideal from the point of view
of that slave driver, Man.[76]

Leo Kennedy commented, in 1976, that "Knister's horses have
more diverse personalities, and are observed more vividly and
acutely than are many human fictional characters that I've stumbled
over or gagged at recently."[77] The vitality Kennedy refers to is
perhaps a reflection of the extent to which Knister evokes both
"equine and human" societies.

As has been mentioned above, Don Precosky compares the poetry
of Knister to that of Carl Sandburg: " . . . his poetry, like Sandburg's,
was regional and realistic."[78] Knister knew and respected the work of
Sandburg:

> . . . if one doubts that free verse should be read aloud let him
> hear, as I did, some of Carl Sandburg's poems. It is strange to
> find the streets and their ugliness, which all men know, con-
> verted into beauty in the soul of a man: one is moved as by the
> highest art, by means impossible of detection. Again, a current
> magazine contains a long poem called *Saint Agnes Eve in Wall
> Street*. It is as different from Keats' poem as the gunman and
> the underworld are from the gods and the Elysian fields. But it
> moves one to hear, spoken in impersonal and level tones, and
> one knows that man must go on exploring his many provinces,
> that his only hope is a truthful and honest search for beauty in
> what experience is given him, in daily life and vision. ("On
> Reading Aloud," p. 14)

There is evidence that this instance of Knister's praise for Sandburg's
work is more than a nod of acknowledgement in passing. Knister's
reading list indicates that between 1921 and 1922 he read Sandburg's
Cornhuskers, a volume of poetry which was published in 1918.
In Knister's poem "Corn Husking," the "cornstalks bow with

laughter" (WC, p. 67). In Sandburg's "Laughing Corn," which is in Cornhuskers, the corn is associated with "a conquering laughter."[79] Sandburg's rather brief poem ends with a reference to "the farm-house," where, it is implied, "the farmer and his wife talk things over together"; in Knister's longer poem, characters speak as they actually work at corn husking. While Sandburg leaves the work of corn husking off-stage, although it is referred to in the last verse of his poem, it is central in Knister's poem. In this regard Knister's poem begins where Sandburg's ends, and Knister's choice of title may reflect a desire to acknowledge such continuity.

Echoes of other poems in Cornhuskers seem to be found in Knister's work, if sometimes adapted to different ends. "Alix," Sandburg's poem of a racehorse (CP, pp. 94–95), can be compared to Knister's "Arab King" (WC, p. 64) in both form and content. Sandburg's poem "Baby Face" (CP, p. 131) features a "White Moon" that seems to function in a way similar to, but not as complexly as, the "White Cat" in Knister's poem of the same title (WC, p. 21). In "Manitoba Childe Roland" (CP, pp. 98–100), the combined presentation of literary tradition and the here-and-now would likely appeal to Knister's literary sensibility. And while Sandburg's "One Modern Poet" did not appear in Cornhuskers, the sensibility it expresses is one that Knister, as the author of "Feed" (WC, p. 20), can be imagined as sharing:

> Having heard the instruction:
>   "Be thou no swine,"
> He belabored himself and wrote:
>   "Beware of the semblance
>   of lard at thy flanks."
>
> (CP, p. 671)

While "Corn Husking" is atypical of Knister's work in being a longer poem, it includes a number of elements that recur in his poetry. The poem covers a day of working at corn husking, as seen from the point of view of the son of the farmer who leads the harvest. "Corn Husking" illustrates the sharpness of Knister's eye for the details that conjure up a particular environment. In giving fragments of good-humoured teasing and gossip, as well as sights and sounds of the working environment, Knister conveys why it is the work does not become grindingly monotonous. "A golden popping like one

hears . . . / In popcorn pans, is seen . . . " (WC, p. 71) as the work
proceeds; there is acknowledgement of the inherent beauty of the
natural world, and in this instance, little alienating distance between
man and his environment, even when tiredness sets in towards the
end of the working day:

> . . . The corn
> Is bent over with the wind in some places,
> And we must stoop quite low to seize each ear.
> Hard on the back it is, a little bit.
> Then Roy begins to hum, and whistle soft,
> "The last Rose of Summer."
> "Give me the last
> Rows of corn," Bill says, "and you can have
> The rose of summer."
>
> (WC, p. 72)

The four corn huskers talk, tease, and observe as they work, and
work becomes a source of satisfaction. There is something tremen-
dously appealing about the harmonious, cooperative working relationships that Knister depicts. Unsentimental good-naturedness
marks the way one corn husker characterizes another:

> . . . Bill
> Is always anxious when night comes on
> Or noon, for that matter . . . .
>
> (WC, p. 73)

Knister's writing can explore experience with integrity, without
foregoing a keen sense of possibility. As James Reaney notes in his
Preface to Windfalls for Cider, "the poems drawn from Knister's
farm experiences" can raise the question, "Is it that the simpler and
more basic the activity, the closer we are to paradise?" (WC, p. 7).

Knister made poetry out of material as diverse as seasonal change,
social climbing, the artistic process, and corn husking. His best
poetry is technically deft and intensely evocative. In being engaged
with reality, Knister's poetry celebrates experience, for all the limita-
tions of everyday life. For Knister, having "the courage of our
experience" gives rise to art:

Nothing, not poetry or dreams, can exist except on the basis of reality. As long as we flinch from contact with the actual, we shall go without great poetry . . . . ("The Poetic Muse in Canada," p. 22)

NOTES

The knowledge and encouragement of David Arnason and James Reaney made the writing of this essay possible. Imogen Knister Givens patiently and kindly answered numerous questions about her father's life and work, and permitted quotation from unpublished material.

[1] For this and subsequent information, I am indebted to Imogen Knister Givens.

[2] Marcus Waddington, "Raymond Knister: A Biographical Note," *Journal of Canadian Fiction*, No. 14 (1975) [Raymond Knister issue], p. 175. All further references to this work (Waddington) appear in the text.

[3] Imogen Givens courteously provided a copy of this list.

[4] "Raymond Knister," an unpublished essay, kindly made available by Imogen Givens. It may have been written by Knister and seems to form the basis for Leo Kennedy's "Raymond Knister," *The Canadian Forum*, Sept. 1932, pp. 459–61.

[5] Anne Burke, "Raymond Knister: An Annotated Bibliography," in *The Annotated Bibliography of Canada's Major Authors*, ed. Robert Lecker and Jack David, III (Downsview, Ont.: ECW, 1981), 292.

[6] David Arnason, "Canadian Poetry: The Interregnum," *CV/II*, 1, No. 1 (Spring 1975), 31. All further references to this work appear in the text.

[7] Bonita O'Halloran, "Chronological History of Raymond Knister," *Journal of Canadian Fiction*, No. 14 (1975) [Raymond Knister issue], p. 194. All further references to this work (O'Halloran) appear in the text.

[8] Raymond Knister, Letter to Elizabeth Frankfurth [copy], 11 April 1924, Raymond Knister Papers, Queen's Univ. Archives, Kingston, Ont.

[9] Ernest Walsh, Letter to Raymond Knister, 23 April 1925, Raymond Knister Papers, Queen's Univ. Archives, Kingston, Ont.

[10] Raymond Knister, Letter to Elizabeth Frankfurth [copy], 19 Nov. 1925, Raymond Knister Papers, Queen's Univ. Archives, Kingston, Ont.

[11] William Murtha, ed. and introd., *Short Stories of Thomas Murtha* (Ottawa: Univ. of Ottawa Press, 1980). The Introduction discusses the friendship of Murtha and Knister.

[12] Desmond Pacey, ed. and introd., *The Letters of Frederick Philip Grove* (Toronto: Univ. of Toronto Press, 1976), pp. 283–84.

[13] Joy Kuropatwa, "A Handbook to Raymond Knister's Longer Prose Fiction," Diss. Western Ontario 1985, pp. 135, 162.

[14] Leo Kennedy, "A Poet's Memoirs," rev. of *Journal of Canadian Fiction*, No. 14 (1975) [Raymond Knister issue], *CV/II*, 2, No. 2 (May 1976), 23–24.

[15] Marcus Waddington, "Raymond Knister and the Canadian Short Story," M.A. Thesis Carleton 1977, p. 223. All further references to this work (Waddington, Thesis) appear in the text.

[16] Imogen Givens, "Raymond Knister — Man or Myth?" *Essays on Canadian Writing*, No. 16 (Fall–Winter 1979–80), pp. 5–19.

[17] Raymond Knister, "Democracy and the Short Story," *Journal of Canadian Fiction*, No. 14 (1975) [Raymond Knister issue], p. 148. All further references to this work appear in the text.

[18] Raymond Knister, "A Great Poet of To-Day, Edwin Arlington Robinson, Author of 'The Man against the Sky,'" *The New Outlook*, 30 June 1926, pp. 6, 27; rpt. in his *The First Day of Spring: Stories and Other Prose*, ed. and introd. Peter Stevens, Literature of Canada: Poetry and Prose in Reprint, No. 17 (Toronto: Univ. of Toronto Press, 1976), p. 417.

[19] Raymond Knister, "Canadian Letter," in Stevens, ed., *The First Day of Spring*, p. 380. All further references to this work appear in the text.

[20] Raymond Knister, "Canadian Literati," *Journal of Canadian Fiction*, No. 14 (1975) [Raymond Knister issue], p. 167. All further references to this work appear in the text.

[21] William Butler Yeats, "Modern Poetry: A Broadcast," in *Essays and Introductions* (New York: Collier, 1968), p. 499.

[22] Raymond Knister, *White Narcissus* (New York: Harcourt, Brace, 1929), p. 189.

[23] Raymond Knister, Foreword, *Windfalls for Cider: The Poems of Raymond Knister*, ed. and introd. Joy Kuropatwa, with a Preface by James Reaney (Windsor, Ont.: Black Moss, 1983), p. 15. All further references to this work (*WC*) appear in the text.

[24] Raymond Knister, "The Poetry of Archibald Lampman," *The Dalhousie Review*, 7 (Oct. 1927), 348–61; rpt. in Stevens, ed., *The First Day of Spring*, p. 456. All further references to this work appear in the text.

[25] Raymond Knister, "The Poetic Muse in Canada," *Saturday Night*, 6 Oct. 1928, p. 3. All further references to this work appear in the text.

[26] Ezra Pound, "Credo," in *Literary Essays of Ezra Pound*, ed. and introd. T. S. Eliot (New York: New Directions, 1968), pp. 9, 10.

[27] Raymond Knister, "The Canadian Short Story," *The Canadian Bookman*, 5 (Aug. 1923), 203–04; rpt. in Stevens, ed., *The First Day of Spring*, p. 390.

[28] Quoted in Dorothy Livesay, "Raymond Knister: A Memoir," in *Collected Poems of Raymond Knister*, ed. Dorothy Livesay (Toronto: Ryerson, 1949), p. xxi. All further references to this work appear in the text.

[29] Raymond Knister, "Katherine Mansfield," in Stevens, ed., *The First Day of Spring*, p. 428.

[30] Rev. of *The Poetical Works of Wilfred Campbell*, ed. W. J. Sykes,

Queen's Quarterly, 31 (May 1924), 435–39; rpt. "The Poetical Works of Wilfred Campbell," in Stevens, ed., *The First Day of Spring*, p. 450.

[11] Knister, "The Canadian Short Story," p. 389.

[12] Raymond Knister, Introd., *Canadian Short Stories* (Toronto: Macmillan, 1928), pp. xi–xix; rpt. in Stevens, ed., *The First Day of Spring*, p. 394.

[13] Henry James, "Preface to 'The American,' " in *The Art of the Novel*, introd. Richard P. Blackmur (New York: Scribner's, 1962), p. 32.

[14] I am indebted to Dr. G. Rans for this observation, and I would like to express my thanks to him for his introduction to, and guidance within, the world of the theory and the practice of nineteenth-century American romance.

[15] Knister, *White Narcissus*, pp. 194–95.

[16] Nathaniel Hawthorne, Preface, *The House of the Seven Gables* (New York: New American Library, 1961), p. vii.

[17] Raymond Knister, "The Lost Gentleman," *Journal of Canadian Fiction*, No. 14 (1975) [Raymond Knister issue], p. 152. All further references to this work appear in the text.

[18] Knister, Introd., *Canadian Short Stories*, p. 394.

[19] Raymond Knister, "The Canadian Girl," *Journal of Canadian Fiction*, No. 14 (1975) [Raymond Knister issue], p. 159.

[40] Raymond Knister, "Canadian Literature: A General Impression," *Journal of Canadian Fiction*, No. 14 (1975) [Raymond Knister issue], p. 171. All further references to this work appear in the text.

[41] Knister, "The Canadian Girl," p. 159.

[42] Raymond Knister, "A Shropshire Lad," in Stevens, ed., *The First Day of Spring*, p. 420.

[43] David Arnason, "The Development of Prairie Realism: Robert J. Stead, Douglas Durkin, Martha Ostenso and Frederick Philip Grove," Diss. New Brunswick 1980, p. 223.

[44] See above, note 12.

[45] Clara Thomas and John Lennox, *William Arthur Deacon: A Literary Life* (Toronto: Univ. of Toronto Press, 1982). See pages 41, 42, 56, 57, 89–92, 144, and 229.

[46] See above, note 11.

[47] Leo Kennedy, *The Shrouding* (Toronto: Macmillan, 1933).

[48] Dorothy Livesay, *Right Hand Left Hand*, ed. David Arnason and Kim Todd (Erin, Ont.: Porcépic, 1977), pp. 48–58.

[49] *The Poet Who Was Farmer Too: A Profile of Raymond Knister*, prod. John Wood and Allan Anderson, CBC Radio, 19 July 1964. Doris Everard included a transcript of this broadcast in Appendix II of her "Tragic Dimensions in Selected Short Stories of Raymond Knister," M.A. Thesis Sir George Williams 1972, pp. 233–68.

[50] See above, note 14.

[51] Earle Birney, *Spreading Time: Remarks on Canadian Writing and Writers, Book I: 1904–1949* (Montreal: Véhicule, 1980), p. 24.

[52] See above, note 16.

[53] Raymond Knister, Letter to his parents, 29 Oct. 1928, Raymond Knister Collection, Mills Memorial Library, McMaster Univ., Hamilton, Ont.

[54] Raymond Knister, Letter to his father, 8 Feb. 1928, Raymond Knister Collection, Mills Memorial Library, McMaster Univ., Hamilton, Ont.

[55] Raymond Knister, Letter to Myrtle Knister, 11 May 1928, Raymond Knister Collection, Mills Memorial Library, McMaster Univ., Hamilton, Ont.

[56] H[erbert] R[ead], "Exiles," rev. of *This Quarter*, *The New Criterion*, 4 (April 1926), 403–04.

[57] Dorothy Livesay, "Knister's Stories," rev. of *Selected Stories of Raymond Knister*, *Canadian Literature*, No. 62 (Autumn 1974), p. 80.

[58] G. H. Clarke, "Recent Poetry," rev. of *Collected Poems of Raymond Knister*, and three other books, *Queen's Quarterly*, 56 (Winter 1949–50), 605–06.

[59] Alan Crawley, "The Red Heart and Raymond Knister," rev. of *The Red Heart*, by James Reaney, and *Collected Poems of Raymond Knister*, *Contemporary Verse*, No. 31 (Spring 1950), p. 21.

[60] Milton Wilson. "Klein's Drowned Poet: Canadian Variations on an Old Theme," *Canadian Literature*, No. 6 (Autumn 1960), p. 5.

[61] Earle Birney, "About Reaney and Knister," rev. of *The Red Heart*, by James Reaney, and *Collected Poems of Raymond Knister* [text of CBC Radio review, 14 Dec. 1949], in *Spreading Time*, p. 154.

[62] Munro Beattie, "Poetry 1920–1935," in *Literary History of Canada: Canadian Literature in English*, 2nd ed., gen. ed. and introd. Carl F. Klinck (Toronto: Univ. of Toronto Press, 1976), II, 240.

[63] Peter Stevens, "The Old Futility of Art: Knister's Poetry," *Canadian Literature*, No. 23 (Winter 1965), p. 46. All further references to this work appear in the text.

[64] George A. Ross, "Three Minor Canadian Poets: Louis Alexander MacKay, Leo Kennedy and Raymond Knister," M.A. Thesis Alberta 1969, p. 68.

[65] Bernhard Beutler, *Der Einfluss des Imagismus auf die moderne kanadische Lyrik englischer Sprache* (Frankfurt am Main: Peter Lang, 1978), p. 48. All further references to this work appear in the text.

[66] Don Precosky, "Ever with Discontent: Some Comments on Raymond Knister and His Poetry," *CV/II*, 4, No. 4 (Spring 1980), 4. All further references to this work appear in the text.

[67] Northrop Frye, "Conclusion," in Klinck, gen. ed., *Literary History of Canada*, II, 358.

[68] Everard, pp. 247–48.

[69] Raymond Knister, "Dissecting the 'T.B.M.': A Reply to S. Laycock's 'Why Be True to Life' and a Ruthless Investigation of a Certain Mental Viewpoint," *Saturday Night*, 6 Sept. 1930, p. 5.

[70] Livesay, "Knister's Stories," p. 81.

[71] See above, note 35.

[72] *The New Outlook*, 13 Oct. 1926, p. 16.

[73] Raymond Knister, "On Reading Aloud," *The New Outlook*, 27 Oct. 1926, p. 14. All further references to this work appear in the text.

[74] Knister, "Dissecting the 'T.B.M.' . . . ," p. 5.

[75] Stevens, Introd., *The First Day of Spring*, p. xviii.

[76] *Journal of Canadian Fiction*, No. 14 (1975) [Raymond Knister issue], p. 108.

[77] Kennedy, "A Poet's Memoirs," p. 24.

[78] See above, note 66.

[79] Carl Sandburg, *Complete Poems* (New York: Harcourt, Brace, 1950), p. 87. All further references to this work (*CP*) appear in the text.

SELECTED BIBLIOGRAPHY

Primary Sources

Letters

Knister, Raymond. Letter to Elizabeth Frankfurth [copy]. 11 April 1924.
Raymond Knister Papers. Queen's Univ. Archives, Kingston, Ont.
——. Letter to Elizabeth Frankfurth [copy]. 19 Nov. 1925. Raymond
Knister Papers. Queen's Univ. Archives, Kingston, Ont.
——. Letter to his father. 8 Feb. 1928. Raymond Knister Collection. Mills
Memorial Library, McMaster Univ., Hamilton, Ont.
——. Letter to Myrtle Knister. 11 May 1928. Raymond Knister Collection.
Mills Memorial Library, McMaster Univ., Hamilton, Ont.
——. Letter to his parents. 29 Oct. 1928. Raymond Knister Collection.
Mills Memorial Library, McMaster Univ., Hamilton, Ont.

Books

Knister, Raymond, ed. and introd. *Canadian Short Stories*. Toronto:
Macmillan, 1928.
——. *White Narcissus*. New York: Harcourt, Brace, 1929.
——. *My Star Predominant*. Toronto: Ryerson, 1934.
——. *Collected Poems of Raymond Knister*. Ed. and with a Memoir by
Dorothy Livesay. Toronto: Ryerson, 1949.
——. *Selected Stories of Raymond Knister*. Ed. and introd. Michael
Gnarowski. Canadian Short Stories, No. 2. Ottawa: Univ. of Ottawa
Press, 1972.
——. *Journal of Canadian Fiction*, No. 14 (1975) [Raymond Knister
issue]. Ed. David Arnason. Rpt. *Raymond Knister: Poems, Stories and
Essays*. Ed. and introd. David Arnason. Montreal: Bellrock, 1975.
Knister, Raymond. *The First Day of Spring: Stories and Other Prose*. Ed.
and introd. Peter Stevens. Literature of Canada: Poetry and Prose in
Reprint, No. 17. Toronto: Univ. of Toronto Press, 1976.
——. *Windfalls for Cider: The Poems of Raymond Knister*. Ed. and
introd. Joy Kuropatwa. Pref. James Reaney. Windsor, Ont.: Black Moss,
1983.

Contributions to Periodicals and Books

Knister, Raymond. "The Canadian Short Story." *The Canadian Bookman*, 5 (Aug. 1923), 203–04. Rpt. in his *The First Day of Spring: Stories and Other Prose*. Ed. and introd. Peter Stevens. Literature of Canada: Poetry and Prose in Reprint, No. 17. Toronto: Univ. of Toronto Press, 1976, pp. 388–92.

— —. Rev. of *The Poetical Works of Wilfred Campbell*, ed. W. J. Sykes. *Queen's Quarterly*, 31 (May 1924), 435–39. Rpt. "The Poetical Works of Wilfred Campbell." In his *The First Day of Spring: Stories and Other Prose*. Ed. and introd. Peter Stevens. Literature of Canada: Poetry and Prose in Reprint, No. 17. Toronto: Univ. of Toronto Press, 1976, pp. 440–54.

———. "A Great Poet of To-Day, Edwin Arlington Robinson, Author of 'The Man against the Sky.'" *The New Outlook*, 30 June 1926, pp. 6, 27. Rpt. in his *The First Day of Spring: Stories and Other Prose*. Ed. and introd. Peter Stevens. Literature of Canada: Poetry and Prose in Reprint, No. 17. Toronto: Univ. of Toronto Press, 1976, pp. 412–19.

— —. "Purposes of Fiction." *The New Outlook*, 13 Oct. 1926, p. 16.

— —. "On Reading Aloud." *The New Outlook*, 27 Oct. 1926, p. 14.

———. "The Poetry of Archibald Lampman." *The Dalhousie Review*, 7 (Oct. 1927), 348–61. Rpt. in his *The First Day of Spring: Stories and Other Prose*. Ed. and introd. Peter Stevens. Literature of Canada: Poetry and Prose in Reprint, No. 17. Toronto: Univ. of Toronto Press, 1976, pp. 454–69.

———. "The Poetic Muse in Canada." *Saturday Night*, 6 Oct. 1928, pp. 3, 22.

———. "Dissecting the 'T.B.M.': A Reply to S. Laycock's 'Why Be True to Life' and a Ruthless Investigation of a Certain Mental Viewpoint." *Saturday Night*, 6 Sept. 1930, p. 5.

———. "Boquet and Some Buds: A Stable Anthology." *Journal of Canadian Fiction*, No. 14 (1975) [Raymond Knister issue], pp. 107–15.

———. "The Canadian Girl." *Journal of Canadian Fiction*, No. 14 (1975) [Raymond Knister issue], pp. 154–59.

———. "Canadian Literati." *Journal of Canadian Fiction*, No. 14 (1975) [Raymond Knister issue], pp. 160–68.

———. "Canadian Literature: A General Impression." *Journal of Canadian Fiction*, No. 14 (1975) [Raymond Knister issue], pp. 169–74.

———. "Democracy and the Short Story." *Journal of Canadian Fiction*, No. 14 (1975) [Raymond Knister issue], pp. 146–48.

———. "The Lost Gentleman." *Journal of Canadian Fiction*, No. 14 (1975) [Raymond Knister issue], pp. 149–53.

—. "Canadian Letter." In his *The First Day of Spring: Stories and Other Prose*. Ed. and introd. Peter Stevens. Literature of Canada: Poetry and Prose in Reprint, No. 17. Toronto: Univ. of Toronto Press, 1976, pp. 377–82.

—. "Katherine Mansfield." In his *The First Day of Spring: Stories and Other Prose*. Ed. and introd. Peter Stevens. Literature of Canada: Poetry and Prose in Reprint, No. 17. Toronto: Univ. of Toronto Press, 1976, pp. 427–35.

—. "A Shropshire Lad." In his *The First Day of Spring: Stories and Other Prose*. Ed. and introd. Peter Stevens. Literature of Canada: Poetry and Prose in Reprint, No. 17. Toronto: Univ. of Toronto Press, 1976, pp. 419–27.

Secondary Sources

Arnason, David. "Canadian Poetry: The Interregnum." *CV/II*, 1, No. 1 (Spring 1975), 28–32.

—. "The Development of Prairie Realism: Robert J. Stead, Douglas Durkin, Martha Ostenso and Frederick Philip Grove." Diss. New Brunswick 1980.

Beattie, Munro. "Poetry 1920–1935." In *Literary History of Canada: Canadian Literature in English*. 2nd ed. Gen. ed. and introd. Carl F. Klinck. Toronto: Univ. of Toronto Press, 1976. II, 239–41.

Beutler, Bernhard. *Der Einfluss des Imagismus auf die moderne kanadische Lyrik englischer Sprache*. Frankfurt am Main: Peter Lang, 1978.

Birney, Earle. "About Reaney and Knister." Rev. of *The Red Heart*, by James Reaney, and *Collected Poems of Raymond Knister* [text of CBC Radio review, 14 Dec. 1949]. In *Spreading Time: Remarks on Canadian Writing and Writers, Book I: 1904–1949*. Montreal: Véhicule, 1980, pp. 153–55.

Burke, Anne. "Raymond Knister: An Annotated Bibliography." In *The Annotated Bibliography of Canada's Major Authors*. Ed. Robert Lecker and Jack David. Vol. III. Downsview, Ont.: ECW, 1981, 281–322.

Clarke, G. H. "Recent Poetry." Rev. of *Collected Poems of Raymond Knister*, and three other books. *Queen's Quarterly*, 56 (Winter 1949–50), 605–06.

Crawley, Alan. "The Red Heart and Raymond Knister." Rev. of *The Red Heart*, by James Reaney, and *Collected Poems of Raymond Knister*. *Contemporary Verse*, No. 31 (Spring 1950), pp. 20–25.

Everard, Doris. "Tragic Dimensions in Selected Short Stories of Raymond Knister." M.A. Thesis Sir George Williams 1972.

Frye, Northrop. "Conclusion." In *Literary History of Canada: Canadian Literature in English*. 2nd ed. Gen. ed. and introd. Carl F. Klinck. Toronto: Univ. of Toronto Press, 1976. II, 333–61.

Givens, Imogen. "Raymond Knister — Man or Myth?" *Essays on Canadian Writing*, No. 16 (Fall–Winter 1979–80), pp. 5–19.

Hawthorne, Nathaniel, preface. *The House of the Seven Gables*. New York: New American Library, 1961, pp. vii–ix.

James, Henry. "Preface to 'The American.'" In *The Art of the Novel*. Introd. Richard P. Blackmur. New York: Scribner's, 1962, pp. 20–39.

Kennedy, Leo. "Raymond Knister." *The Canadian Forum*, Sept. 1932, pp. 459–61.

————. *The Shrouding*. Toronto: Macmillan, 1933.

————. "A Poet's Memoirs." Rev. of *Journal of Canadian Fiction*, No. 14 (1975) [Raymond Knister issue]. *CV/II*, 2, No. 2 (May 1976), 23–24.

Kuropatwa, Joy. "A Handbook to Raymond Knister's Longer Prose Fiction." Diss. Western Ontario 1985.

Livesay, Dorothy. "Raymond Knister: A Memoir." In *Collected Poems of Raymond Knister*. Ed. Dorothy Livesay. Toronto: Ryerson, 1949, pp. xi–xli. Rpt. (revised) in *Right Hand Left Hand*. Ed. David Arnason and Kim Todd. Erin, Ont.: Porcépic, 1977, pp. 48–58.

————. "Knister's Stories." Rev. of *Selected Stories of Raymond Knister*. *Canadian Literature*, No. 62 (Autumn 1974), pp. 79–83.

Murtha, William, ed. and introd. *Short Stories of Thomas Murtha*. Ottawa: Univ. of Ottawa Press, 1980, pp. 13–31.

O'Halloran, Bonita. "Chronological History of Raymond Knister." *Journal of Canadian Fiction*, No. 14 (1975) [Raymond Knister issue], pp. 194–99.

Pacey, Desmond, ed. and introd. *The Letters of Frederick Philip Grove*. Toronto: Univ. of Toronto Press, 1976.

The Poet Who Was Farmer Too: A Profile of Raymond Knister. Prod. John Wood and Allan Anderson. CBC Radio. 19 July 1964. Archives Disc. 640719–10.

Pound, Ezra. "Credo." In *Literary Essays of Ezra Pound*. Ed. and introd. T. S. Eliot. New York: New Directions, 1968, pp. 9–12.

Precosky, Don. "Ever with Discontent: Some Comments on Raymond Knister and His Poetry." *CV/II*, 4, No. 4 (Spring 1980), 3–9.

R[ead], H[erbert]. "Exiles." Rev. of *This Quarter*. *The New Criterion*, 4 (April 1926), 403–04.

Ross, George A. "Three Minor Canadian Poets: Louis Alexander MacKay, Leo Kennedy and Raymond Knister." M.A. Thesis Alberta 1969.

Sandburg, Carl. *Complete Poems*. New York: Harcourt, Brace, 1950.

Stevens, Peter. "The Old Futility of Art: Knister's Poetry." *Canadian Literature*, No. 23 (Winter 1965), pp. 45–52.

Thomas, Clara, and John Lennox. *William Arthur Deacon: A Literary Life*. Toronto: Univ. of Toronto Press, 1982.

Waddington, Marcus. "Raymond Knister: A Biographical Note." *Journal of Canadian Fiction*, No. 14 (1975) [Raymond Knister issue], pp. 175–92.

————. "Raymond Knister and the Canadian Short Story." M.A. Thesis Carleton 1977.

Walsh, Ernest. Letter to Raymond Knister. 23 April 1925. Raymond Knister Papers. Queen's Univ. Archives, Kingston, Ont.

Wilson, Milton. "Klein's Drowned Poet: Canadian Variations on an Old Theme." *Canadian Literature*, No. 6 (Autumn 1960), pp. 5–17.

Yeats, William Butler. "Modern Poetry: A Broadcast." In *Essays and Introductions*. New York: Collier, 1968, pp. 491–508.